animalsanimals

Rabbits

by **Melissa Stewart**

Marshall Cavendish
Benchmark
New York

Marshall Cavendish Benchmark
99 White Plains Road
Tarrytown, New York 10591-9001
www.marshallcavendish.us

Library of Congress Cataloging-in-Publication Data

Stewart, Melissa.
Rabbits / by Melissa Stewart.
p. cm. — (Animals animals)
Summary: "Describes the physical characteristics, habitat, behavior, life
cycle, and conservation status of the rabbit"—Provided by publisher.
Includes bibliographical references and index.
ISBN-13: 978-0-7614-2528-1
1. Rabbits—Juvenile literature. I. Title. II. Series.

QL737.L32S74 2006
599.32—dc22
2006019717

Photo research by Candlepants Incorporated

Cover photo: Digital Vision Ltd / SuperStock

The photographs in this book are used by permission and through the courtesy of:
Corbis: Herbert Kehner/zefa, 1; D. Robert & Lorri Franz, 10; Herbert Spichtinger/zefa, 17. *Peter Arnold, Inc.:* B. Fischer, 4;
Francisco Marquez, 6; Manefred Danegger, 12; Diane Shapiro, 13; Steven Kazlowski, 28; Cyril Ruoso, 36;
John Cancalosi, 42. *Minden Pictures:* Edwin Giesbers/Foto Natura, 9, 22, 27; Jim Brandenburg, 16, 30. *Animals Animals:*
Steven David Miller, 14; Lynn Stone, 39; Zigmund Leszcynski, 26. *Getty Images:* Tim Shepard, Oxford Scientific Films, 20;
Bob Elsdale, 33; Hulton Archive, 38. *Super Stock:* age fotostock, 32, 24; Creatas, 34; Ron Dahlquist, 40.

Printed in Malaysia
6 5 4 3 2 1

Contents

1 Introducing Rabbits

As the setting sun casts long shadows across a grassy meadow, an eastern cottontail hops out from under a bush. The rabbit has been napping all day, and now it is hungry.

The cottontail lifts its head and twitches its nose as it sniffs the air. There is no sign of danger, so the rabbit bounds over to a patch of lush green grass and starts nibbling.

As the rabbit eats, it stays alert. Its large ears slowly pivot, or move, to pick up even the softest sounds. Between bites, the cottontail lifts its head and scans the meadow. For rabbits, the world can be a dangerous place.

A cottontail rabbit has many predators, so it is always on the lookout for danger.

A rabbit's long ears can pick up even the softest sounds.

Even though rabbits have many *predators*, they have managed to survive on Earth for 30 million years. Today, more than twenty different *species*, or kinds, of rabbits live in fields and forests, deserts and wetlands around the world. Rabbits live on every continent except Antarctica.

6

For many years, scientists thought they had identified all the different rabbit species on Earth. But in 1998, an automatic camera set up in a tropical forest.

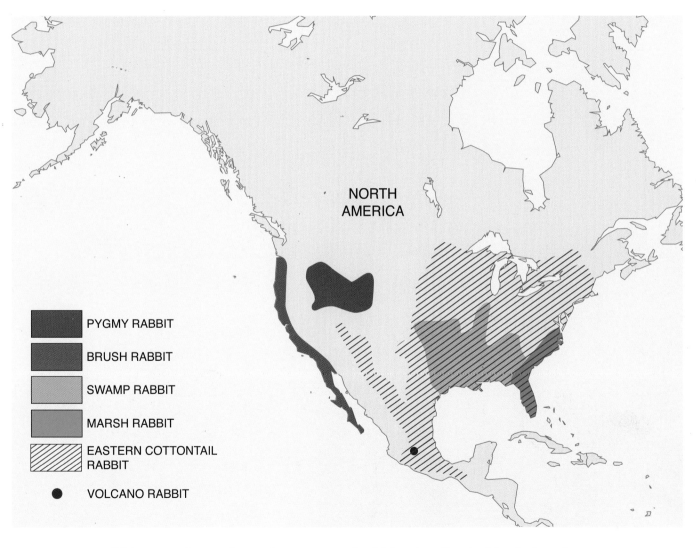

PYGMY RABBIT

BRUSH RABBIT

SWAMP RABBIT

MARSH RABBIT

EASTERN COTTONTAIL RABBIT

● VOLCANO RABBIT

NORTH AMERICA

This map shows the major groups of rabbits that live in North America.

Species Chart

◆ Bushman rabbits live in the Karroo Desert of South Africa. They have very long ears and soft, silky fur.

◆ Central African rabbits live in Angola, Burundi, the Central African Republic, Chad, Kenya,

A European rabbit.

◆ If you have ever spotted a rabbit in the wild, it was probably one of the fourteen species of cottontails found in a wide variety of North American *habitats.* A desert cottontail is pictured on the left. Can you guess how the cottontail got its name? The white, fluffy fur on the underside of its tail looks like a bouncing cotton ball when the rabbit hops away.

◆ Pygmy rabbits live among large clumps of *sagebrush* in the western United States. They are small and have short, rounded ears. Because they have short back legs, they scamper across the ground instead of hopping like other rabbits.

◆ Three different species of red rabbits live in rocky areas or at the edge of forests in southern Africa. They have short legs and thick, woolly fur.

◆ Ryukyu rabbits live on two small islands in Japan. They have long bodies and thick, woolly fur.

◆ Volcano rabbits live in pine forests on a few mountains near Mexico City, Mexico. They have short, rounded ears and no tail.

in the Annamite Mountains in Vietnam snapped a surprising photo. It showed a species of rabbit scientists had never seen before. The red-rumped Annamite rabbit has short ears, black-and-brown-striped fur on its sides, and a reddish back end. Maybe scientists will discover more new rabbit species in the future.

Rabbits have a lot in common with their close relatives, the hares, but there are some important differences. Hares are usually larger than rabbits. In the wild, rabbits range from 10 to 18 inches (25 to 46 centimeters) long and weigh between 1 and 5 pounds

Rabbits are agile, able to run fast and leap through the air.

(0.5 to 2.5 kilograms). An average hare is about 24 inches (61 centimeters) long and can weigh as much as 12 pounds (5 kilograms). Hares usually have longer legs, ears, and tails than rabbits do.

The best way to tell whether an animal is a rabbit or a hare is to look at its young. A baby hare is called a *leveret.* It is born with its eyes open and a full coat of fur. The teeth are ready to start nibbling grass a few days later. It can run and hop just a few hours after birth.

A baby rabbit, called a *kitten,* has a different start in life. It is born blind and deaf. It has no teeth and no fur. For the first few weeks of life, a rabbit kitten relies on its mother for almost everything.

2 A Rabbit's Habits

It is early morning in a calm and silent Georgia swamp. Heavy, humid air hangs over the shallow water. It is going to be another hot day.

Kerplunk! A sudden splash ripples the water near a clump of cattails. It is a marsh rabbit. The little animal wants one last dip in the cool water before it heads off to sleep. The rabbit closes its nostrils tight and dives below the surface. When it comes up for air, the rabbit paddles around for a few minutes and then swims to shore.

After shaking itself dry, the marsh rabbit hops into the tall reeds. It clears the plants from a small patch of ground and digs a shallow hole. The hollow will

Like other rabbits, this marsh rabbit is usually active in the early morning and late evening. It sleeps most of the day.

Like the marsh rabbit, this swamp rabbit is a kind of cottontail that likes water and spends most of its time in wetlands.

make a perfect sleeping spot. Safe and well-hidden, the rabbit settles down for a snooze. To stay cool as the sizzling sun beats down, the rabbit releases extra body heat through the blood vessels in its ears.

When the rabbit wakes a few hours later, it spends some time *grooming*. It licks its fur to remove insects, dirt, and bits of dead skin. Then it naps some more.

All across North America, other kinds of rabbits are also sleeping the day away. Except for the pygmy rabbit, which digs its own burrow, North American rabbits sleep and nest alone in protected areas above ground.

This rabbit is grooming, or cleaning, its fur.

Did You Know . . .

Many small animals *hibernate* during the winter, but rabbits stay active all year long. Their long, soft fur keeps them warm. During cold weather, less blood flows through rabbits' ears. This helps them keep as much body heat as possible.

The Rabbit:

A rabbit's curved backbone and large back feet . . .

Inside and Out

. . . make it possible for these agile animals to leap out of harm's way.

A European rabbit sits close to the entrance of the warren where it lives with many other rabbits.

European rabbits are more social. Groups of these rabbits live together in *warrens*—large underground networks of burrows and tunnels. They dig tunnels using their short front legs.

Like cottontails, European rabbits usually feed in the early morning and late afternoon. All rabbits spend several hours a day grazing on grass and munching on leaves. They may also eat seeds and roots.

Like many animals that eat plants, a rabbit has wide, flat back teeth for grinding its food. It also has two pairs of teeth called *incisors*—one behind the other—at the front of its mouth. These teeth are perfect for snipping off the tastiest parts of plants. A rabbit's incisors never stop growing, so it must gnaw on bark and twigs to wear them down.

A rabbit's *digestive system* is perfectly designed for taking in large amounts of plant material. *Bacteria* living in a rabbit's *intestines* break down the toughest plant parts, so *nutrients* can pass into the rabbit's blood.

But the bacteria are not perfect. They let some important nutrients slip by. During the day, when a rabbit is resting, it releases soft waste pellets. The animal then eats the pellets. That way the bacteria in the rabbit's intestines get a second chance to draw out the nutrients in the material. Later, the rabbit releases a second set of hard, dry pellets.

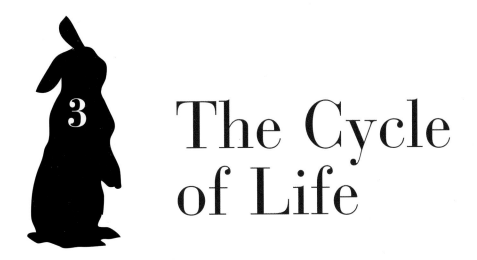

The Cycle
of Life

3

It is early March in the foothills of northern California, and a male brush rabbit, or *buck*, is looking for a mate. As the buck feeds each night, he looks and listens for signs of a female.

When the male spots a female rabbit, or *doe*, he chases her into a clearing. The rabbits hop around each other and leap high into the air. They even playfully box or fight using their front paws. Then the male grooms the female, and the rabbits nuzzle.

After the pair mates, the buck hops off in search of another female. But the doe must get ready for the birth of her babies. Each night, she spends extra time feeding. The babies growing inside her need a lot of

When a male rabbit finds a female, they can then mate and produce young.

A mother cottontail with her young in their fur-lined nest.

energy to develop. The doe's body becomes heavier and heavier. She begins to have trouble moving around.

After about a month, the babies are ready to be born. The doe builds a warm, soft nest of dried grasses and leaves. She lines it with fur she has plucked from her sides and belly. A few hours later, she gives birth to up to six tiny rabbit kittens. Their ears and eyes are closed, and their furless bodies shiver. The doe covers them with pieces of fur and grass, and then quickly hops away.

The mother isn't deserting her babies or leaving them behind. She is trying to keep them safe. Predators can smell an adult rabbit, but the babies have no scent. By staying away from the nest, the mother decreases the chances that a hungry animal will find her hidden youngsters.

A few times each night, the mother returns to the nest to feed her babies. She approaches it in a zigzag pattern and then leaps the last few feet in a single jump. That way she does not leave a scent trail that predators can follow.

Rabbits are *mammals* like dogs and cats, mice and monkeys, horses and humans. All baby mammals drink milk that their mothers make inside their bodies. When the little rabbit kittens have had their fill, the mother hops away. She will not return until the next feeding time.

When the babies are about a week old, they begin to grow fur. After two weeks, thick fur

Did You Know . . .
If a rabbit manages to stay safe, it can live up to ten years.

covers their entire bodies. By then, the youngsters can see and hear well. When they are three weeks old, the young rabbits begin to leave the nest and explore.

By the time the youngsters are a month old, they have begun to eat plants. They spend several hours each day playing near the nest. When they are tired,

This litter of rabbit kittens is feeding on its mother's milk.

Young rabbits stick close to their mother.

A young rabbit must learn to be alert if it is to make it through its first year.

they snuggle together and fall asleep. Soon they will be old enough to go off on their own. For now, they live as a group.

A female brush rabbit can have up to five *litters* each year, but other kinds of cottontails may have as many as eight. With up to eight kittens in each litter, a single doe can have more than sixty babies a year. Some of the rabbits she gives birth to will have babies of their own before the summer ends.

With so many babies being born each year, you might wonder why there are not more rabbits in the world. Only one in ten rabbit kittens makes it to its first birthday. It is not easy to survive in a habitat full of hungry predators.

4 That Rascally Rabbit

Eagles, hawks, and owls swoop down from the sky. Foxes, bobcats, and coyotes leap out of the thick grass or from behind bushes. Snakes and weasels sneak into nests, burrows, or other sleeping spots. With so many predators, it is not surprising that so few rabbits survive their first year of life. Even as adults, rabbits must always be on the lookout for danger.

To survive in the wild, rabbits use their highly developed senses. They also rely on a few special tricks. Like most plant eaters, a rabbit's eyes are on the sides of its head. As a rabbit grazes on grasses and other plant material, it can look far to the left, right, and all around.

This great horned owl has caught a rabbit. The little mammal will make a good meal.

As this European rabbit sits at the entrance to its warren, it pivots its ears in every direction. It wants to know if predators are nearby before it hops out into the open.

A rabbit's funnel-shaped ears can twist and swivel in any direction. While one ear turns to the right, the other turns to the left.

This movement helps rabbits pick up sounds too quiet for people to hear. Rabbits can also feel vibrations in the ground. This helps them detect predators closing in on foot.

In a flash, this rabbit darts into tall grass. With powerful legs, rabbits are designed for making quick escapes when a predator is about.

*Can this rabbit outrun
the gray wolf that
wants it for its dinner?*

When a rabbit senses a predator nearby, it quickly thumps on the ground with one of its feet to warn other rabbits. Then it crouches close to the ground and stays frozen and still. Because many predators look for movement, they may have trouble spotting the rabbit.

If the predator does not leave the area, the rabbit jumps up and runs away in a zigzag pattern. This makes it hard for the predator to follow. The rabbit continues to dodge and dart until it reaches the safety of tall grass or thick bushes. A rabbit's muscular back legs give it the power to run at speeds of up to 25 miles (40 kilometers) per hour.

If a hungry predator manages to catch its *prey*, the rabbit lets out an ear-piercing squeal. Sometimes the terrible noise startles the hunter so much that it drops the rabbit. Then the little animal quickly runs away and hides.

5 Rabbits and People

The rabbit's long list of predators includes humans. People have been hunting and eating rabbits for thousands of years. In cooler parts of the world, people also used rabbit fur to make coats, gloves, and hats.

The ancient Romans raised wild rabbits in pens and ate them at feasts. Soldiers and explorers who wanted a sure source of food took rabbits with them to other parts of the world.

About one thousand years ago, French monks began to tame European rabbits. By the 1500s, people had developed different kinds of *domestic*, or tamed, rabbits. While some domestic rabbits are still eaten and used to make clothing, most are kept as pets or for medical research.

This rabbit has found a good spot to hide from a hunter.

Pet rabbits are gentle, curious creatures. They can form strong bonds with people as well as other pets. They are easy to care for and feed, and can even be trained to use a litter box.

This woman is spinning wool from the fur of her angora rabbits.

This domestic rabbit has unusually short ears.

If you live in the country or just outside a city, you may have seen wild rabbits in a field or wooded area. Maybe you have even seen them in your own backyard. While few people mind rabbits nibbling at their lawns, the hungry mammals can do a lot of harm to a family garden. Just imagine what would happen to a farmer's crops or your own home-grown

39

Even though the Australian government has tried to control the country's rabbit population, its efforts have not been successful. With no natural predators, rabbit numbers keep rising year after year.

vegetables if rabbits did not have any natural predators.

People living in Australia do not have to imagine. They know exactly how much trouble rabbits can cause. In 1859 twenty-four European rabbits were let loose by a farmer who wanted to hunt them. Without any natural predators, the rabbits *multiplied* quickly. By 1900 rabbits were eating crops and grassy pastures across Australia. Hunters shot as many rabbits as they could, but they could not kill enough to stop the rabbit population from growing.

By 1950 the Australian government realized it had to take steps to control the number of rabbits. Scientists released a virus that harmed rabbits, but did not affect other animals. The virus worked well in some parts of the country, but not as well as the Australian government had hoped. Later, the disease was accidentally introduced to Europe. Thousands of rabbits died in Great Britain, Belgium, and France as a result.

While Australia still struggles with its large rabbit population, rabbits are actually having trouble surviving in other parts of the world. As people cut down trees for firewood and building materials or clear land for farms, buildings, and parking lots, many of the

No one wants rabbits to disappear from Earth forever. By working together to protect the places where rabbits live, we can be sure they will always be around.

places where rabbits live are being destroyed. In North America, the marsh rabbit and volcano rabbit are in danger of disappearing. Several African species are also at risk.

Rabbits have lived on Earth for millions of years. During that time, they have learned to survive in a variety of places. But without healthy habitats, their future may not be so bright. People must work together to protect the natural areas that still exist. That way rabbits and many other creatures will be able to survive well into the future.

Glossary

bacteria—Tiny, one-celled living things that reproduce by dividing. Some kinds of bacteria live in the intestines of rabbits and other animals.

buck—A male rabbit.

digestive system—The parts of the body involved in breaking down food and moving nutrients into the blood.

doe—A female rabbit.

domestic—Tamed and living with people.

groom—To clean fur or feathers.

habitat—The place where a plant or animal lives.

hibernate—To spend the winter resting. When animals hibernate, their body functions slow down.

incisors—Sharp front teeth used for cutting.

intestines—The part of the digestive system that breaks down food particles and allows nutrients to pass into the blood.

kitten—A baby rabbit.

leveret—A baby hare.

litter—A group of young animals born at the same time to the same mother.

mammal—A warm-blooded animal that has a backbone and hair, and feeds its young milk the mother makes.

multiply—To grow or increase.

nutrients—Sugars, proteins, minerals, and other materials that an animal's body needs to grow and stay healthy.

predator—An animal that hunts and kills other animals for food.

prey—An animal that is hunted by a predator.

sagebrush—A short, dense shrub that grows in the western United States.

species—A group of similar creatures that can mate and produce healthy young.

warren—A network of underground tunnels and dens built by rabbits.

Find Out More

Books

Barnes, Julia. *101 Facts about Rabbits*. Milwaukee, WI: Gareth Stevens, 2003.

Boring, Mel. *Rabbits, Squirrels and Chipmunks*. Minocqua, WI: NorthWord Press, 2000.

Gibbons, Gail. *Rabbits, Rabbits & More Rabbits*. New York: Holiday House, 2000.

Hinds, Kathryn. *Rabbits*. Tarrytown, NY: Benchmark Books, 1999.

Jacobs, Lee. *Rabbits*. San Diego, CA: Blackbirch Press, 2002.

Miller, Sara Swan. *Rabbits, Pikas, and Hares*. New York: Franklin Watts, 2002.

Tagholm, Sally. *The Rabbit*. New York: Kingfisher, 2000.

Trumbauer, Lisa. *The Life Cycle of a Rabbit*. Mankato, MN: Pebble Books, 2004.

Web Sites

Animal Hospitals USA—Rabbits
http://www.animalhospitals-usa.com/small_pets/
    rabbits.html

Fresno Chaffee Zoo—Rabbits
http://www.chaffeezoo.org/animals/rabbit.html

The Humane Society—Rabbits
http://www.hsus.org/wildlife/a_closer_look_at_wildlife/
    rabbits.html

Rabbits and Rabbit Care
http://www.rabbit.org/faq/

About the Author

Melissa Stewart has a bachelor's degree in biology from Union College and a master's degree in science and environmental journalism from New York University. She has written more than seventy children's books and numerous articles about animals, ecosystems, earth science, and space science.

Index

Page numbers for illustrations are in **boldface**.